ARTHUR KORN

GLASS

IN MODERN ARCHITECTURE
of the Bauhaus Period

GEORGE BRAZILLER

Produced by Design Yearbook Limited, 21 Ivor Place,
London N.W.1.
Originally published in German under the title *Glas im Bau
und als Gebrauchsgegenstand* in 1926
Text set by Harrison & Sons Limited, 20-22 Bedfordbury
London W.C.2.
Reproduction by Compton Printing Limited, Pembroke Road,
Stocklake, Aylesbury, Buckinghamshire.
Printed by Taylor, Garnett, Evans Limited, Bushey Mill Lane,
Watford, Hertfordshire.

For information address the publisher:
George Braziller Inc., One Park Avenue, New York, N.Y.
10016.
Library of Congress Catalog Card Number: 68-11357.
This edition first published 1968.

Printed in England.

CONTENTS

FOREWORD Dennis Sharp

This book was originally published in 1929 under the title, *Glas im Bau und als Gebrauchsgegenstand,* by the Berlin publisher Ernst Pollak.

The book's appearance in 1929 was timely. The Werkbund had held its highly successful exhibition of housing projects at the Weissenhof Settlement in Stuttgart two years earlier and the formation of CIAM had taken place at La Sarraz the previous year. Both these events contributed to a consolidation of the ideas for a 'new practicality' in architecture.

Arthur Korn's superb picture book of the buildings of that period offers an invaluable record of the achievements of the architects who saw a great potential in the use of glass and concrete. Korn was deeply committed to the new architecture and his book displays a perceptive awareness of the work that was going on all round him. Korn's keen eye for masterly building, the well designed detail and the beautiful object can be seen in the selection of the illustrations which range from a simple lamp bulb from Pintsch to the ambitious projects of the Russian Constructivist architects. In between, the now familiar buildings of the Heroic Period are featured: Mies van der Rohe's glass architecture projects and his apartment block for the Weissenhof Exhibition; Le Corbusier and Pierre Jeanneret's houses; the first stage of the Van Nelle factory at Rotterdam by Brinkmann and Van der Vlugt; buildings and projects by the Luckhardt Brothers, Otto Haesler, Oldrich Tyll of Prague and most significantly the outstanding tuberculosis sanatorium at Hilversum by the Dutch architect J. Duiker. Characteristically there are no 'doubtful modern' buildings in this book and no overtly fanciful designs among the projects. The buildings illustrated show the purity of the so-called 'International Style' of the late twenties in which ornament had been successfully eliminated, eclecticism cured and a simple, yet bold geometrical basis accepted for architectural form. With the designers' desire for simplicity, glass offered remarkable possibilities. It opened up interior and external space, it offered large reflective surfaces, a clean finish, the window wall, and a screen for night illumination.

Apart from the numerous illustrations of contemporary buildings and projects Korn also included in his book a number of articles, written by specialists, on *Luxfer* glass prisms, glass mosaics and glass painting. Although they were of considerable importance in the first edition they have been omitted from this present volume because of their technical nature and because developments in glass construction since the twenties have outdated them. However, the illustrations are still pertinent.

In the same year that Korn's book appeared, K. W. von Schulze published his *Glas in der Architektur der Gegenwart* which also indicated the interest and trust architects had in a material that could be turned to real creative use. Both books showed the use of glass as a logical extension of the ideas that were implied almost eighty years earlier in Paxton's Crystal Palace. The architect had, almost paradoxically, become the creative engineer—a mechanistic aesthetician. The material itself was not without poetry, and Korn remarks in his introduction that 'glass is an altogether exceptional material, at once reality and illusion, substance and shadow: it is there yet it is not there.' A similar but rather more romantic interest in glass as a building material had been advocated by avant-garde circles in Berlin immediately after the First World War. Bruno Taut, the virtual leader of the extremist architectural front in the post-war period, had demonstrated the design possibilities of glass in his domed pavilion, erected for the German glass industry, at the Werkbund Exhibition at Cologne as early as 1914. He had found a mentor in the old Expressionist poet Paul Scheerbart who dreamt of a day when a new glass architectural paradise would become reality. Scheerbart's vision was of an highly coloured environment of thick glass walls, glass floors, glass ceilings and stairs. He published his ideas in a little book called *Glasarchitektur* in 1914, claiming that architecture should be freed from the confines of rigidly enclosed spaces. 'We can only do this' he wrote, 'by introducing a glass architecture that admits the sunlight, the moonlight, and the light of the stars into the room . . . through as many walls as possible, which are to consist entirely of glass—coloured glass.'

Arthur Korn's views clearly owe something to the intense interest generated by Taut and his colleagues of the Berlin Glass Chain Group in glass construction, but he had little sympathy with the romantic dreams its participants shared. His sympathy was—and still is—with the triumph of an idea in practical reality. His book is a testimony of such an achievement in his own work and in that of his contemporaries.

INTRODUCTION Arthur Korn

To this edition

When this book was written about forty years ago outstanding buildings like the Barcelona Pavilion (1929) by Mies Van der Rohe or the Boot's Factory, Nottingham (1932) by Sir Owen Williams did not yet exist. Yet it contained the best buildings in glass by Mies, e.g., the competition Friedrichstrasse, Berlin (1922), a mushroom construction planned in free-shaped curves and a dreamlike exhibition of coloured plate-glass rooms for an annexe to the Weissenhof-siedlung in Stuttgart (1927).

Since then, glass buildings have appeared all over the world, particularly in the U.S.A. and England. The Vickers Tower, Castrol House and New Zealand House in London to mention just a few together with the United Nations Building, the Seagram and Lever Buildings in New York have changed the character of the existing Towns.

The use of glass has become a mass-phenomenon most significant in the design of shops and in the 'prestige' vestibules to the new office blocks producing what Lissitzky would have called 'Infinite Space'. 'The continuity of space is thus established in a singular way in contrast to all other materials'.

The three-dimensional effect which was established some forty years ago as a new and outstanding feature of glass has become more conscious to-day and it is to be expected that further developments towards the potential qualities of this material may discover new possibilities in the near future.

To the first edition

Glass is an extraordinary material. It gave us the beauty of mediaeval stained glass windows. Tightly held between supporting piers they opened a door to allow a glimpse of paradise in luminous colours from the shadow of the grave.

Nothing has been lost from the richness of those earlier creations, but glass has now been associated with other materials to meet new functions. A new glass age has begun, which is equal in beauty to the old one of Gothic windows.

Up to the present time glass has been a secondary building material, which remained subservient in spite of all its intrinsic ornamental strength, in spite of its crucial position in the interplay of structural forces, in spite of its underlining contrast with the masonry of the walls. The contribution of the present age is that it is now possible to have an independent wall of glass, a skin of glass around a building; no longer a solid wall with windows. Even though the window might be the dominant part—this window is the wall itself, or in other words, this wall is itself the window. And with this we have come to a turning point. It is something quite new compared to the achievements through the centuries . . . it is the disappearance of the outside wall—the wall, which for thousands of years had to be made of solid materials, such as stone or timber or clay products. But in the situation now, the outside wall is no longer the first impression one gets of a building. It is the interior, the spaces in depth and the structural frame which delineates them, that one begins to notice through the glass wall. This wall is barely visible, and can only be seen when there are reflected lights, distortions or mirror effects.

Thus the peculiar characteristic of glass as compared to all materials hitherto in use becomes apparent: glass is noticeable yet not quite visible. It is the great membrane, full of mystery, delicate yet tough. It can enclose and open up spaces in more than one direction. Its peculiar advantage is in the diversity of the impression it creates. Only in recent years has it been realised that this material opens quite a new range of possibilities to the architect. A few examples may illustrate what I mean. If we take, for example, the Bauhaus in Dessau by Walter Gropius, or the buildings by Mies van der Rohe, or the design for the Kopp & Joseph shop by Arthur Korn, we notice quite different aims behind the use of glass.

1) In the office block by Mies van der Rohe (p.12) and the workshop at Dessau (p. 17) the visible depth behind the thin skin of glass is the exciting factor.

2) In the curved office block by Mies van der Rohe (p. 10), the strength of the outer skin with its reflections and mirror effects, as well as the curvature of the smooth glass surface as such, is predominant.

3) With the Kopp & Joseph shop by Arthur Korn, apart from the spatial articulation, the strong colour effects behind an invisible screen are specially emphasised. Here the glass skin is no longer of any visual importance but purely a medium to form a barrier against the weather etc.

When looking at these various possiblities we realise that new rules are at work here, different from those of the past. Glass has an extraordinary quality which enables it to render an outside wall practically non-existent, when one compares such a wall to those made of other materials—stone, wood, metal or marble—all of which form solid barriers.

Obviously, the opening up and perforation of a wall has been an aim and a problem for a considerable time and in some instances solutions were found which even made the interior of a building visible from without, but never before did man succeed in enclosing and dividing up space by a single membrane. It is this membrane which really encloses a building, but only with certain qualities of a solid wall, such as defence against temperature variation and noise, as well as the provision of safety. This is not a purely imaginary wall as it is in the case of the regular rhythm of columns around a classical temple.

It is evident that a material of such qualities requires the building itself to be remodelled, conceived in a revolutionary way. The building by Mies van der Rohe, a structure of unusual and perfect clarity, is based on new and different rules for the use of glass. There is evidence of a new structural concept where all load-bearing elements are kept within the core of the building, leaving the outside wall free to be nothing but a wrapping to enclose and to allow light to penetrate. This function is just the peculiar characteristic of glass, which in this formula shows itself to be at the same time a medium for the penetration of light and a skin for a building, reflecting the sparkling of its own lights and heightening the effect through the occasional glimpses of the load-bearing supports in its interior.

Even if the intensity of colour effects of the new neon lights compete with the strength of those of the old Gothic windows, they are both two-dimensional coloured surfaces only. The new characteristic of glass is evident only when it opens up views deep into the inside of the building, thus exploiting its peculiar property through its position. It is only here that it can show in all its purity the strength of this sophisticated, yet in a way simple, characteristic. Compared with this special and individual property, all other effects of glass—colourful, brilliant and stimulating—are of secondary importance.

The disappearance of the outside wall of a building has its counterpart in a similar process inside. Partitions dissolve into glass walls. This can be observed in various examples, as for instance in the girls' hostel in Prague by Tyll (p. 50) where one passes glass partition after glass partition and meets the same fullness of light inside as in the street outside. Where solutions like this are also coupled to a process of eliminating as many solid walls as possible in the core of a building, delicate structures emerge such as the house for the co-operative by Le Corbusier (p. 19) or the sanatorium at Hilversum by Duiker (p. 55).

The qualities of the architectural concept which have proved both new and lasting have also been evident in the approach to the designing of shops. Here again the tendency to utilise the two-storey skin effect for visual penetration into depth offered possibilities other than the flatness of former shop windows.

Novel developments followed in the area of large-scale advertisements and hoardings in the townscape. Today, it is possible to show these to similar advantage by daylight and during the night with the aid of glass bricks and large sections of sheet glass which can be covered by signs and lettering up to fifty feet high. These large glass surfaces can glow with a diffuse light by night as in the staircase tower in Magdeburg by Carl Krayl (p. 46), where the large signs hardly impede the penetration of daylight. With the help of these large glass surfaces it is now possible to have much greater freedom for advertising designs which hitherto had to be hemmed in between the spandrel panels below window cills.

The window as the structural element of the large glass surface had to be redesigned from basic principles. This was done not only because of the general tendency to reconsider and redesign each of the few basic elements of the modern building, but also because the window is the most exposed element in an outside wall, and furthermore, because a window has to be moveable with a frame as thin as possible. This is the reason why quite a number of new window constructions appeared on the market—both casement and sliding windows. One of these new constructeins is shown in the example by a Swiss architect (Artaria & Schmidt p. 69). With the advance of glass as a building material its use for other purposes also increased. Apart from its extensive use for light fittings, it is being used for the sake of its intrinsic beauty, its hygenic, hard and protective surface in conjunction with furniture of various kinds. The glass table by Marcel Breuer (p. 120) is a good example in this connection. But glass is also used for the manufacture of cooking utensils in the form of fire-proof dishes and other glassware, including intensely refined test tubes and complicated laboratory glass vessels, and these show the wide scope of its use and its form. It is just in these admirable shapes and forms that we see how much we can still expect if one day men are to succeed in extending these creations into the realm and dimension of large buildings with suspended pipes in spirals and glass tubes to take staircases and escalators.

The object of writing this book was to point to new opportunities which are still dormant in glass. The technical details of how these may be put into practice can be left to the experts to put into words.

MIES VAN DER ROHE. PROJECT: A GLASS SKYSCRAPER,
1920-21. MODEL.

10

MIES VAN DER ROHE. PROJECT: THE ADAM BUILDING,   BERLIN, 1928.

12

ABOVE: MIES VAN DER ROHE. PROJECT: GLASS AND STEEL
                OFFICE BUILDING FOR THE FRIEDRICHSTRASSE,
                BERLIN. 1919.

ABOVE LEFT: MIES VAN DER ROHE. PROJECT: BANK BUILDING,
                STUTTGART, 1928.

LEFT: MIES VAN DER ROHE. PROJECT: AN OFFICE BLOCK IN
                REINFORCED CONCRETE AND GLASS. 1922.

WALTER GROPIUS. BAUHAUS, DESSAU. VIEW FROM NORTH.

WALTER GROPIUS. BAUHAUS BUILDINGS, DESSAU. 1926.
INTERIOR OF ADMINISTRATIVE BLOCK.

14

WALTER GROPIUS. BAUHAUS, DESSAU. WORKSHOP WING.

WALTER GROPIUS. BAUHAUS, DESSAU. WORKSHOP WING.

WALTER GROPIUS. OFFICE BUILDING, WERKBUND
EXHIBITION, COLOGNE, 1914 (DESTROYED).

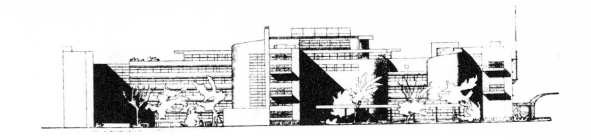

LE CORBUSIER AND PIERRE JEANNERET. CENTROSOYUS
BUILDING, MOSCOW. 1928. (PROJECT 1.)

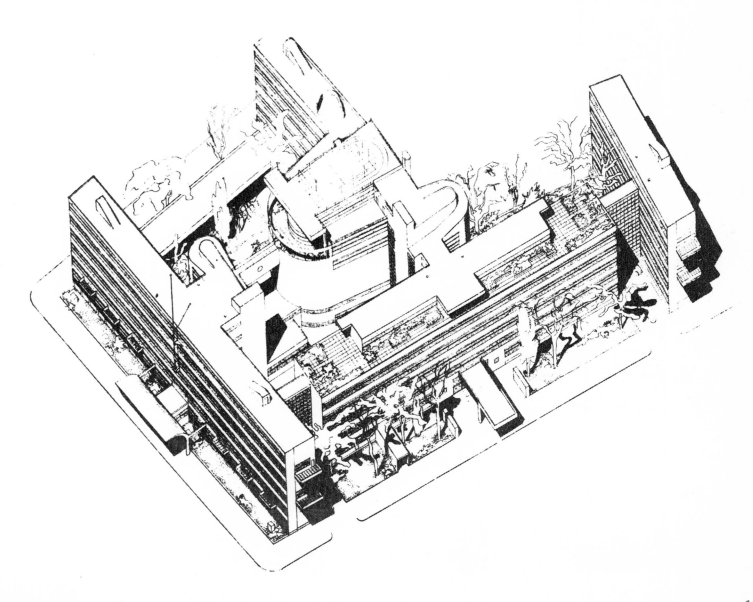

FACTORY, HASTINGS, MICHIGAN, U.S.A.

J. A. BRINKMANN AND L. C. VAN DER VLUGT. VAN NELLE TOBACCO FACTORY, ROTTERDAM. 1928–30.
UNDER CONSTRUCTION.

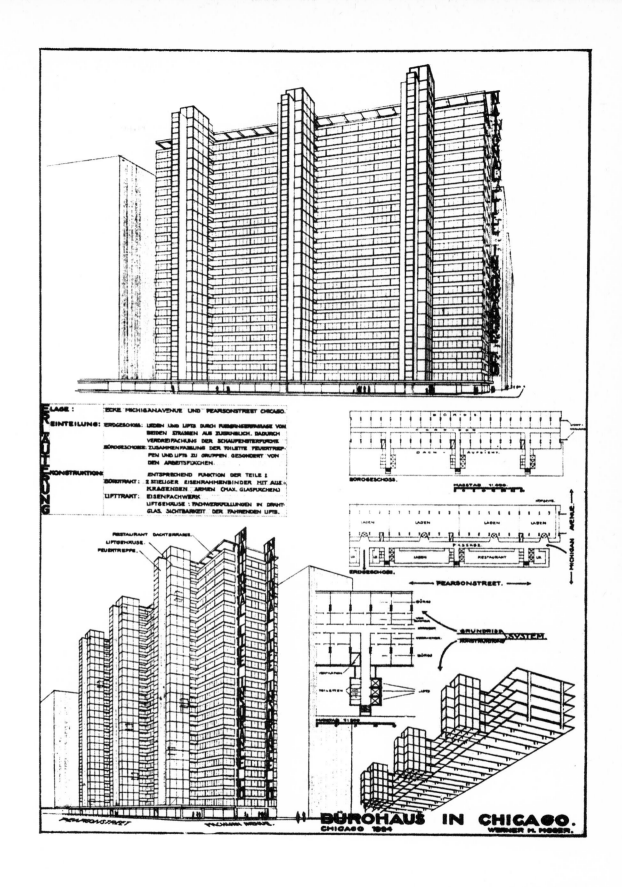

WERNER H. MOSER. PROJECT: CHICAGO OFFICE BUILDING. 1924.

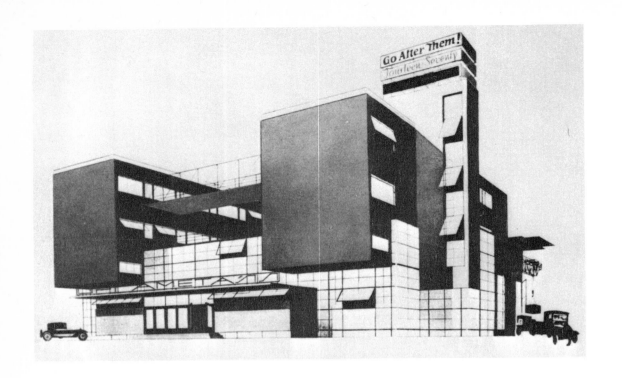

M. GINSBURG. FACTORY AND OFFICE PROJECTS.

W. A. AND A. A. VESNIN. PROJECT:
DEPARTMENT STORE, MOSCOW.

BOHUSLAV FUCHS. SHOP
AND OFFICES, BRUNN.

TOP:
ARTHUR KORN AND SIGFRIED WEITZMANN. OFFICE
BUILDING PROJECT FOR FROMM, FRIEDRICHSTRASSE,
BERLIN, C. 1927.

J. W. S. BUYS. 'DE VOLHARDING'
CO-OPERATIVE BUILDING, THE HAGUE.

ERICH MENDELSOHN. COMPETITION PROJECT: MOSSE
PAVILION, THE PRESS EXHIBITION, COLOGNE, 1928.

ARTHUR KORN, AND SIGFRIED WEITZMANN. MIDDLE
SECTION OF A BUSINESS CENTRE, HAIFA, 1924.

WASSILI AND HANS LUCKHARDT AND ALFONS ANKER.
PROJECT: OFFICES, TAUENTZIENSTRASSE, BERLIN, 1925.

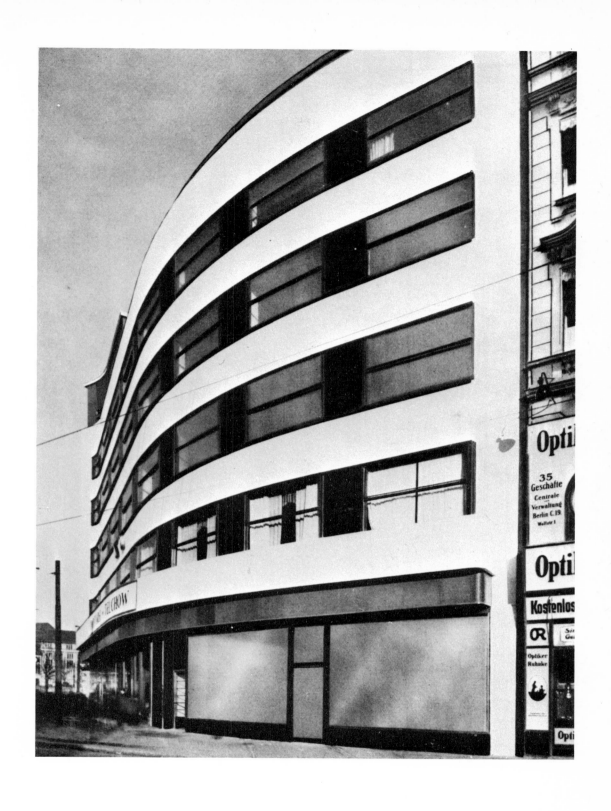

WASSILI AND HANS LUCKHARDT AND ALFONS ANKER.
TELSCHOW HOUSE, BERLIN, 1929.

KÖNIGIN-BAR   EINGANG   GEROLD

WASSILI AND HANS LUCKHARDT AND ALFONS ANKER.
KÖNIGIN-BAR AND OFFICE BUILDING, KURFÜRSTENDAMM,
BERLIN, 1929.

WASSILI AND HANS LUCKHARDT AND ALFONS ANKER.
OFFICE BUILDING, TAUENTZIENSTRASSE, BERLIN, 1925.

BRUNO PAUL. SINN DEPARTMENT STORE, GELSENKIRCHEN.
THE FACADE IS IN GREEN OPAQUE-GLASS.

RICHARD DÖCKER. SHOP AND OFFICES FOR 'LUZ' ELECTRICS, STUTTGART.

ADOLF RADING. MOHREN PHARMACY, BRESLAU. ABOVE : ROOF LEVEL.

ABOVE:
THE NATIONAL PAVILIONS AT THE PRESS
EXHIBITION, COLOGNE, 1928.

BELOW:
HANS SCHUMACHER. ADGB PAVILION, PRESS
EXHIBITION, COLOGNE, 1928.
LEFT: WEST SIDE. RIGHT: INTERIOR.

TOP LEFT: HANS SCHUMACHER. ADGB PAVILION, PRESS EXHIBITION, COLOGNE, 1928. VIEW FROM THE COURTYARD.
LEFT: JIRI KROHA. EXHIBITION PAVILION, BRUNN.
ABOVE: B. PNIEWSKI AND S. SIENICKI. EXHIBITION ENTRANCE, WARSAW.

AUGSBURGER BUNTWEBEREI. CEILING IN LUXFER-TILES.

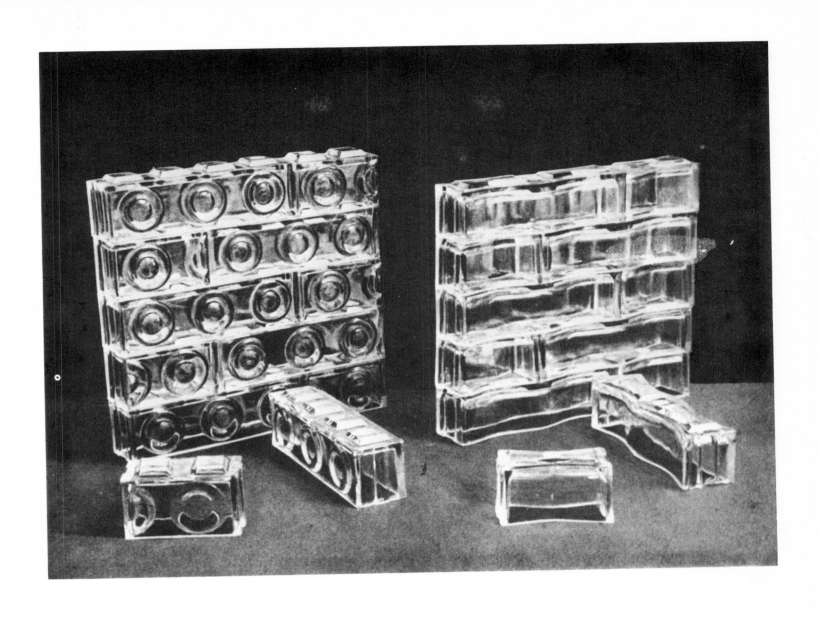

GLASS BRICKS MADE OF MOULDED GLASS BY THE A. G.
FÜR GLASFABRIKATION.

GERMAN RAILWAYS. OVERHEAD LIGHTING TO THE KÖNIGSSTRASSE
SUBWAY, STUTTGART-CANNSTATT.
LEFT: VIEW FROM ABOVE.

CARL KRAYL. LOCAL HEALTH INSURANCE BUILDING,
MAGDEBURG.

LOCAL HEALTH INSURANCE BUILDING, MAGDEBURG. INTERIOR OF PUBLIC HALL.

OTTO HAESLER. GYMNASIUM, SCHOOL, CELLE, 1927.

48

JAN WILS. OLYMPIC STADIUM, AMSTERDAM, 1928.

OLDRICH TYLL. GIRLS' HOSTEL, PRAGUE. VIEW OF THE
LARGE WINDOW IN THE HALL.

GIRLS' HOSTEL, PRAGUE. EXTERIOR.

OLDRICH TYLL. GIRLS' HOSTEL, PRAGUE. VIEW FROM THE
HALL TOWARDS THE GALLERY.

GIRLS' HOSTEL, PRAGUE. CANTEEN.

H.P.BERLAGE. CHURCH
OF CHRIST SCIENTIST,
THE HAGUE, 1925.

VIEW OF SIDE WALL
SHOWING GLASS
BRICKS.

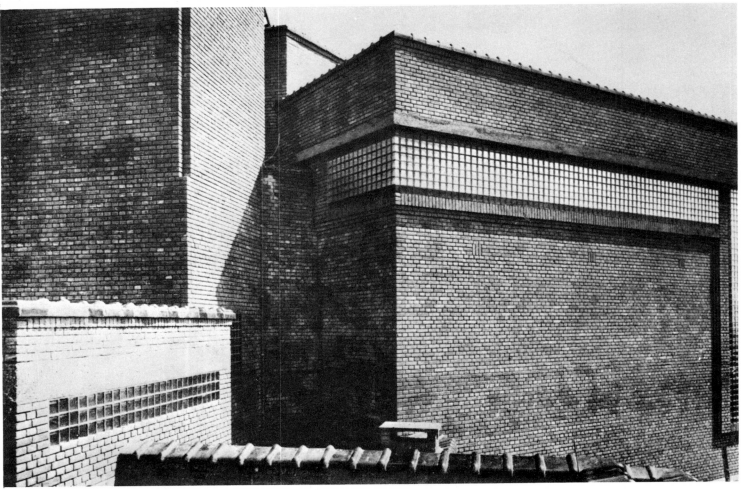

J. DUIKER. *ZONNESTRAAL* SANATORIUM, HILVERSUM, 1928.

LEFT, ABOVE: J. DUIKER. *ZONNESTRAAL* SANATORIUM, HILVERSUM.

OLDRICH TYLL. MARKET BUILDING, PRAGUE.

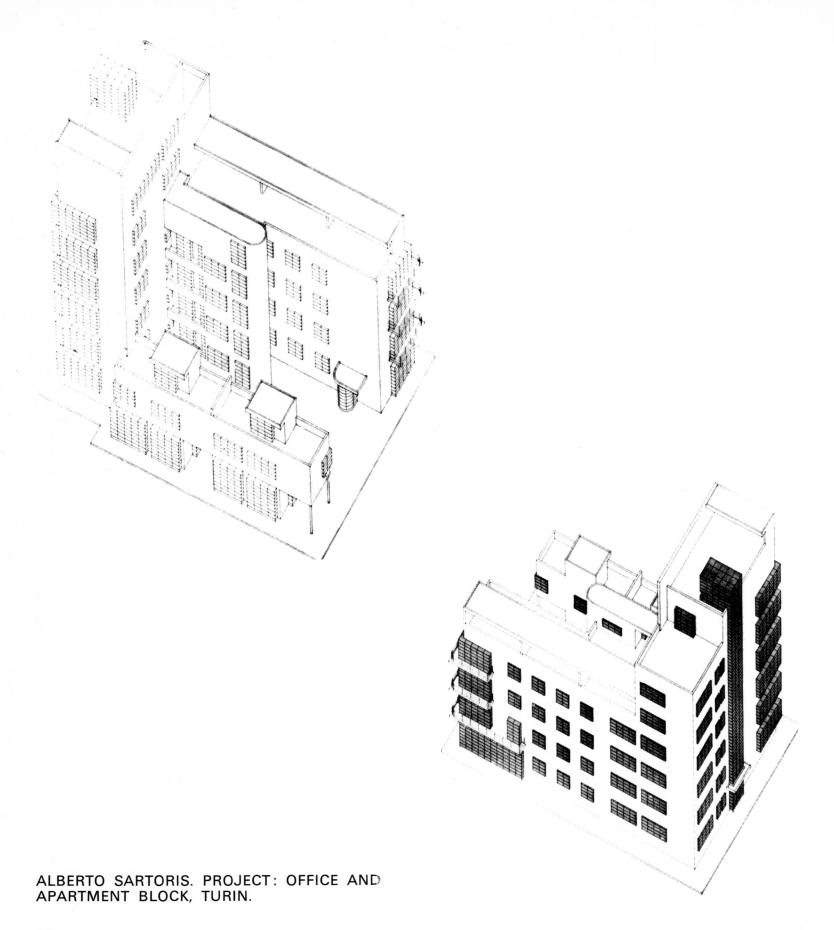

ALBERTO SARTORIS. PROJECT: OFFICE AND
APARTMENT BLOCK, TURIN.

58

MIES VAN DER ROHE. APARTMENT BUILDING, WEISSENHOFSIEDLUNG, STUTTGART, 1927.

MART STAM. ROW HOUSES, WEISSENHOFSIEDLUNG, STUTTGART, 1927.

LE CORBUSIER AND PIERRE JEANNERET. HOUSES, WEISSENHOFSIEDLUNG, STUTTGART, 1927.

LE CORBUSIER AND PIERRE JEANNERET. HOUSE, LAKE OF GENEVA.

63

LE CORBUSIER AND PIERRE JEANNERET. MAISON LA ROCHE, AUTEUIL, 1923.

HALL OF MAISON LA ROCHE.

LE CORBUSIER AND
PIERRE JEANNERET.
SEMI-DETACHED
HOUSES,
WEISSENHOFSIED
LUNG,
STUTTGART, 1927.

LE CORBUSIER AND
PIERRE JEANNERET.
COUNTRY HOUSE.

ABOVE: LE CORBUSIER AND PIERRE JEANNERET.
STUDIO HOUSE FOR OZENFANT,   PARIS, 1922.
RIGHT : STUDIO.

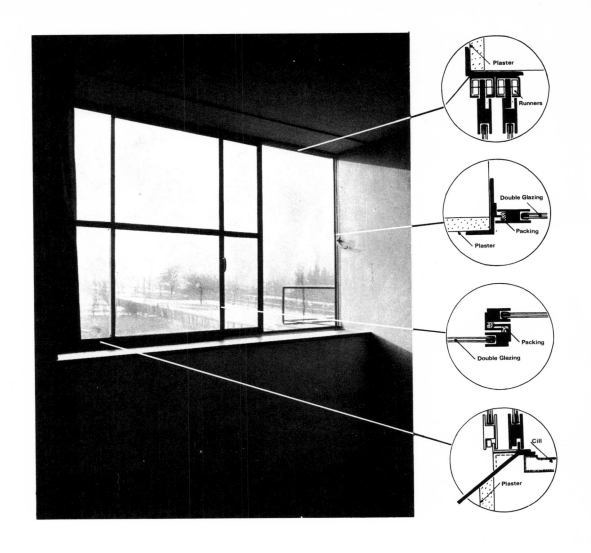

STEEL SASH-WINDOW. PROTOTYPE BY ARTARIA AND
SCHMIDT, ARCHITECTS, BASEL. MANUFACTURER:
A. VOLKMER, BASEL.
LEFT: ARTARIA AND SCHMIDT. HOUSE AT RIEHEN, NEAR
BASEL. THE FIRST USE OF NORMAL SASH-WINDOWS IN
'ELIS' GLAZING. BELOW: WINDOW AND DOOR ON TO
TERRACE.

GERRIT RIETVELD. 'ZAUDY' SHOP, WESEL, GERMANY,
1928 (DESTROYED).

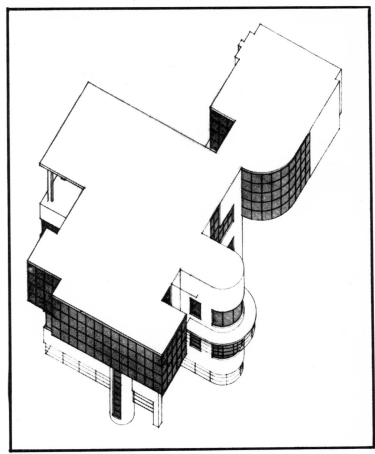

ALBERTO SARTORIS. PROJECT: HOUSE, TURIN.

OTTO HAESLER. COUNTRY HOUSE, CELLE.

OTTO HAESLER. COUNTRY HOUSE, CELLE.

FRANZ ROECKLE   (FRANKFURT-AM-MAIN)
WORKERS' HOUSING,   ESCHERSHEIM.

ERWIN GUTKIND. CHILDRENS' HOME, LICHTENBERG.

ERWIN GUTKIND. CHILDRENS' HOME, LICHTENBERG.   INTERIOR.

HANS SCHAROUN. HOUSE, WEISSENHOFSIEDLUNG, STUTTGART, 1927.

ERWIN GUTKIND. PART OF A HOUSING ESTATE, BERLIN.

KARL SCHNEIDER. RÖMER HOUSE, ALTONA.

JOSEPH FUCHS.
EXHIBITION PAVILION,
BRUNN.

MUNICIPAL BUILDING OFFICES,
FRANKFURT-AM-MAIN.
ELECTRICITY WORKS.

SURROUND OF THE LIGHT- WELL OF THE BIJENKORF DEPARTMENT
STORE, THE HAGUE, 1926.

OTTO BARTNING.
CHILDRENS' HOME.

UNIVERSITY CHILDRENS' CLINIC, TÜBINGEN. ISOLATION WARD.

WASSILI AND HANS LUCKHARDT
AND ALFONS ANKER.
SHOP INTERIOR FOR S. KAUFMANN.

EXHIBITION ROOM, THANNHÄUSER
ART GALLERY, BERLIN, 1926.

ARTHUR KORN AND SIGFRIED WEITZMANN. SHOP
FOR KOPP AND JOSEPH, BERLIN, 1928. FACADE
IN OPAQUE- GLASS.

ARTHUR KORN AND SIGFRIED WEITZMANN. SHOP FOR KOPP AND
JOSEPH, BERLIN.

NIGHT VIEW.

E. AND O. FUCKER.
MUSIC AND PHOTOGRAPHIC SHOP,
FRANKFURT-AM-MAIN,

EXTERIOR VIEW AT NIGHT.

PUBLIC BUILDING DEPARTMENT, FRANKFURT-AM-MAIN. BOOKING HALL.

GERRIT RIETVELD. JEWELLERY SHOP, KALVERSTRAAT, AMSTERDAM, 1920–1922, (DESTROYED).

RIPHAHN AND GROD. SHOP FOR ROSENBERG, COLOGNE.

RIPHAHN AND GROD. INTERIOR OF ROSENBERG SHOP.

KARL SCHNEIDER. HAMMERSCHLAG STORE, HAMBURG.

P. BAUMANN.
SHOPS IN COLOGNE.

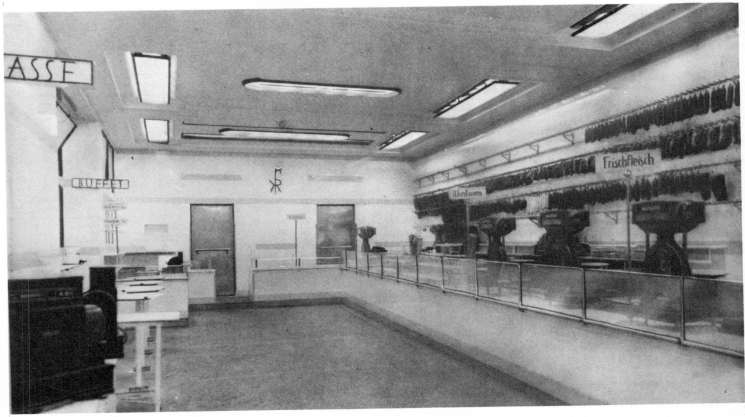

MIES VAN DER ROHE. PLATE-GLASS DISPLAY STAND, GLASS EXHIBITION.

MIES VAN DER ROHE. PLATE-GLASS DISPLAY STAND, GLASS EXHIBITION.

WASSILI AND HANS LUCKHARDT AND ALFONS ANKER.   DINING ROOM.

KARL SCHNEIDER (HAMBURG). MICHAELSOHN HOUSE, FALKENSTEIN.
VIEW FROM LIVING ROOM.

ROBERT MALLET-STEVENS. SWIMMING BATH.

VON WERSIN,
EXHIBITION HALL, MUNICH.

G. KROKA. RESTAURANT, PRAGUE.

MAIN RESTAURANT, THE PRESS EXHIBITION, COLOGNE, 1928. VIEW TOWARDS CATHEDRAL.

LEFT: ALOIS SPALEK (PRAGUE).
HLAVA'S INSTITUTE, MICROSCOPY ROOM, PRAGUE.
GLASS ROOF OVER THE HALL OF THE PHILIPS WORKS, EINDHOVEN.

MIES VAN DER ROHE. INTERIOR OF APARTMENT BLOCK, WEISSENHOFSIEDLUNG. STUTTGART, 1927

LEFT: MUNICIPAL BUILDING AUTHORITY, FRANKFURT-AM-MAIN. GARAGE.
ERNST MAY. HOUSE INTERIOR, FRANKFURT-AM-MAIN.

KREJCAR. INTERIOR OF STORE, PRAGUE.

ALTONA. UPPER CORRIDOR.
KARL SCHNEIDER (HAMBURG). RÖMER HOUSE,

STRAUMER. RADIO TOWER
RESTAURANT, BERLIN.

OTTO HAESLER.
CLASSROOM,
SCHOOL IN CELLE.

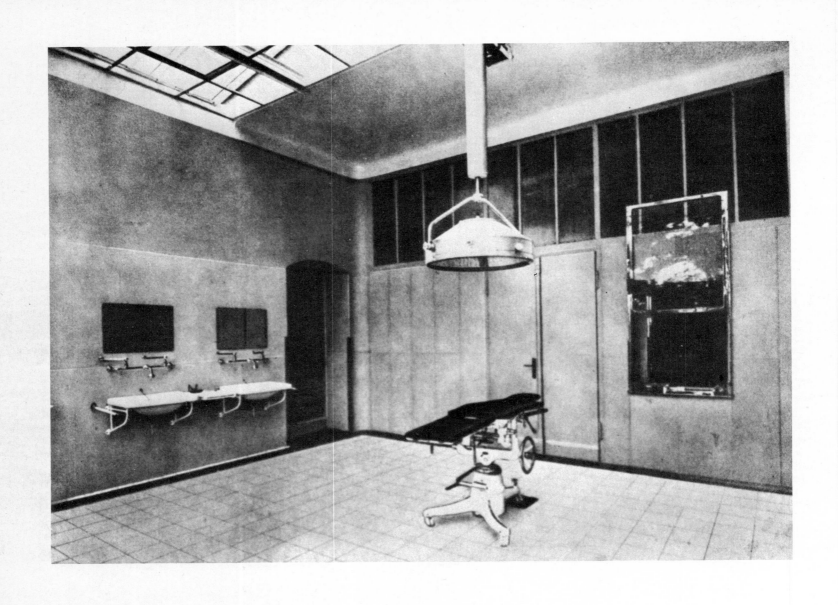

MINISTRY OF PUBLIC BUILDINGS, BRUNSWICK. NATIONAL HOSPITAL, BRUNSWICK. OPERATING THEATRE IN OPAQUE-GLASS.

BRUNO PAUL. GLASS EXHIBITION DISPLAY. OPERATING THEATRE IN OPAQUE-GLASS.

BRUNO PAUL. GLASS EXHIBITION STAND. LABORATORY HALL.

INTERIOR OF THE GERMAN NATIONAL BANK, KÖNIGSBERG.

ARTHUR KORN AND SIGFRIED WEITZMANN. KOPP AND JOSEPH'S SHOP, GLASS DISPLAY UNITS.

KARL SCHNEIDER (HAMBURG) INTERIOR OF SHOP FOR HAMMERSCHLAG.

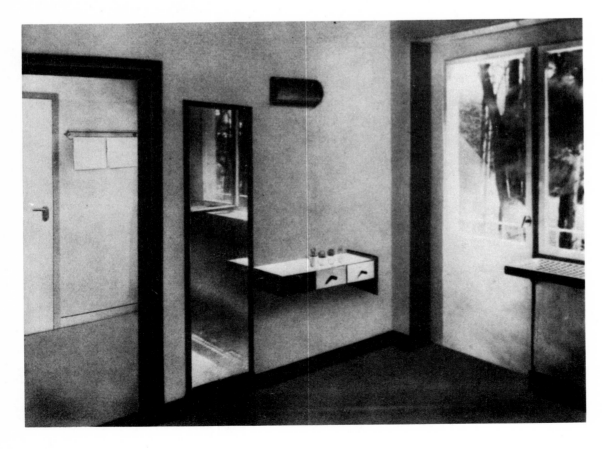

WALTER GROPIUS. LADIES' DRESSING TABLE AND FITTINGS. BAUHAUS, DESSAU.

WASSILI AND HANS LUCKHARDT AND ALFONS ANKER. GLASS CUPBOARDS.

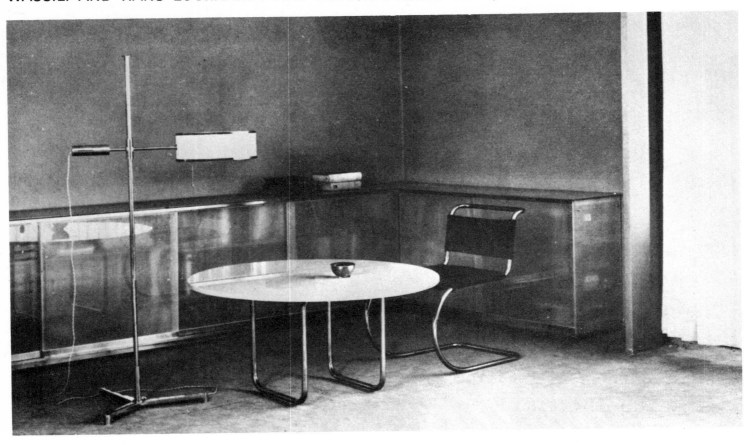

CZECHO-SLOVAKIAN
EXHIBITION, PARIS.
GLASS CUPBOARD.

ARTHUR KORN AND
SIGFRIED WEITZMANN.
MIRROR- GLASS
FRONTED CUPBOARD.

MARCEL BREUER, STEEL AND GLASS TABLE.

THÜRING SCHMUCKGLAS

BRUNO PAUL. GLASS EXHIBITION. VIEW OF PART OF CENTRAL HALL.

BRUNO PAUL. GLASS EXHIBITION. DISPLAY STAND FOR BOTTLES
AND FLASKS.

BRUNO PAUL. STAND AT GLASS EXHIBITION.

BRUNO PAUL. SCIENTIFIC GLASSWARE.

RIGHT: BRUNO PAUL. DISPLAY STANDS FOR VARIOUS PIECES
OF FUNCTIONAL GLASSWARE.
LEERDAM FACTORY. TWO PIECES OF FUNCTIONAL GLASSWARE.

CESAR KLEIN DECORATIVE MOSAIC.

LEFT: PUHL AND WAGNER, GOTTFRIED HEINERSDORFF. BLACK AND
GREY WALL MOSAIC.
PUHL AND WAGNER, GOTTFRIED HEINERSDORFF. MOSAIC TILES AND
MOSAIC CUBES.

GABRIEL GUEVREKIAN. MOSAIC GARDEN FOR THE
HOUSE OF THE VICOMTE DE NOAILLES, HYERES.

JOSEF ALBERS. GLASS PICTURE IN WHITE ON BLACK.

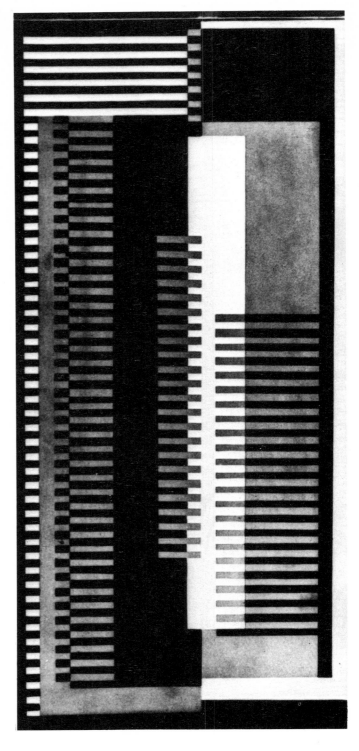

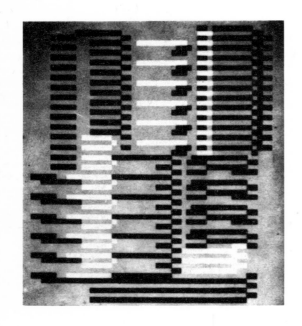

JOSEF ALBERS.   PICTURES ON SHEET GLASS.

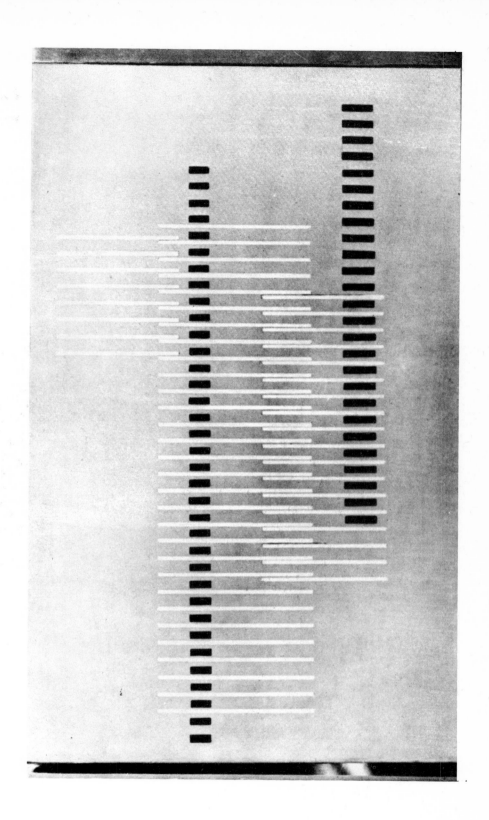

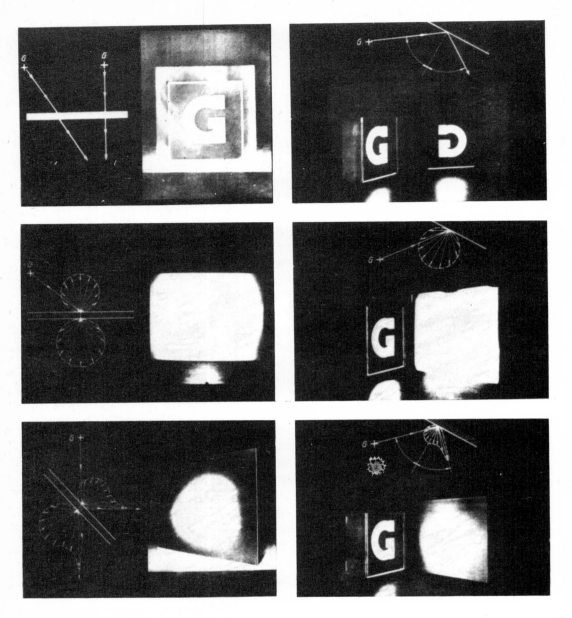

THE PROPERTIES OF VARIOUS MATERIALS USED IN GLASS TECHNOLOGY.

LEFT HAND COLUMN
      DIRECT TRANSMISSION, NO DISPERSION (e.g. CLEAR
      GLASS)

      DIFFUSE TRANSMISSION, GOOD DISPERSION (e.g. GOOD
      OPAL GLASS)
      PARTIAL TRANSMISSION, MEDIUM DISPERSION (e.g.
      GROUND GLASS)

RIGHT HAND COLUMN
      MIRROR REFLECTION (e.g. MIRROR GLASS)
      DIFFUSE REFLECTION (e.g. GROUND OPAL GLASS,
      ALMOST COMPLETE DIFFUSION)
      PARTIAL REFLECTION (e.g. DECORATIVE GLASS)

ENTRANCE HALL LIGHTING. OVERHEAD LIGHTING DURING
THE DAYTIME. THE SAME IMPRESSION IS GIVEN AT NIGHT
WITH LIGHTING UNITS ARRANGED ABOVE THE
EFFICIENT LIGHT DISPERSING CEILING (OPAL GLASS).

ENTRANCE HALL LIGHTING. BY DAY FROM OVERHEAD
LIGHTING (LEFT HAND SIDE OF PICTURE) AND AT NIGHT
FROM ARTIFICIAL OVERHEAD LIGHTING (RIGHT HAND SIDE).

500-VOLT ELECTRIC LIGHT BULB BY PINTSCH.

ARTHUR KORN AND SIGFRIED WEITZMANN. TABLE LAMP
WITH STANDARD GREEN SHADE.

136

BRUNO PAUL. GLASS EXHIBITION, STUTTGART, 1929, OPTICAL ROOM.

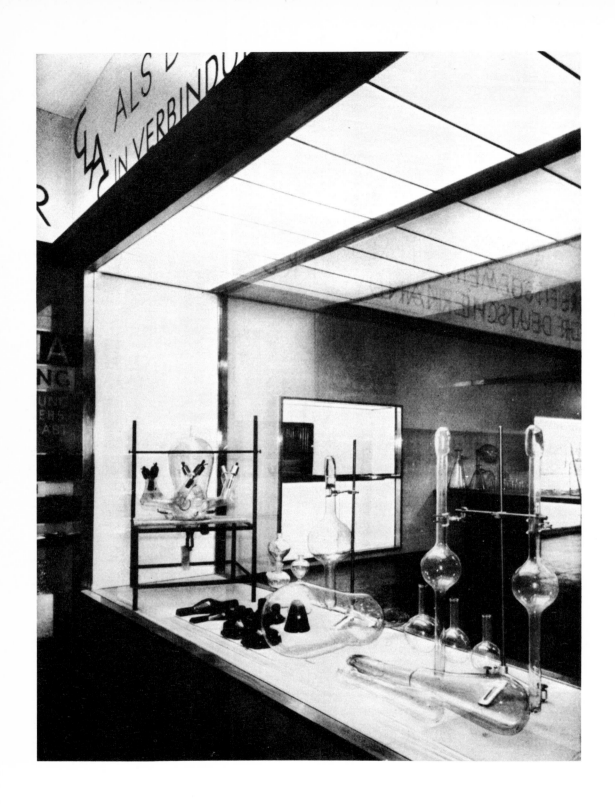

BRUNO PAUL. GLASS EXHIBITION, ROOM FOR CHEMICAL GLASSWARE.

NATIONAL TECHNICAL SCHOOL FOR GLASS INSTRUMENT
TECHNOLOGY, ILMENAU. LARGE BLOWN GLASS CONDENSING COIL.

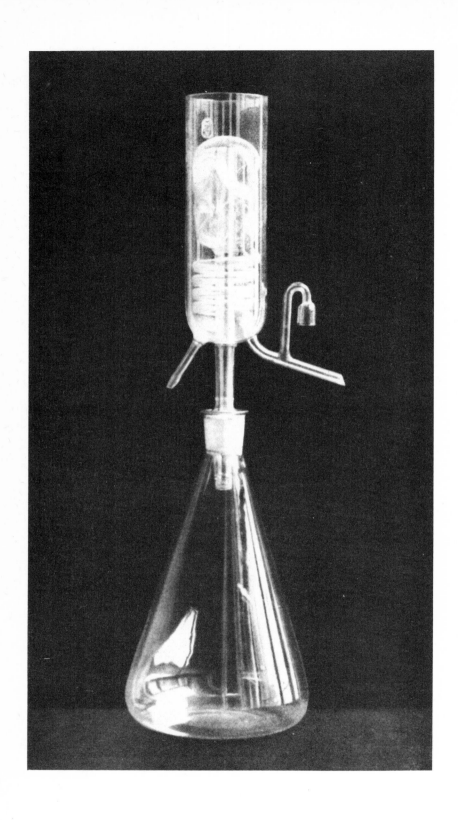

NATIONAL TECHNICAL SCHOOL FOR GLASS INSTRUMENT
TECHNOLOGY. ILMENAU. GLASSWARE.

NAUM GABO. BALLET SET FOR SERGE DIAGHILEFF.